Houck, Louis, 1840–
1925.

The boundaries of
the Louisiana
Purchase

DATE			
OCT 11 '82			
NOV 15 '82			

The First

American Frontier

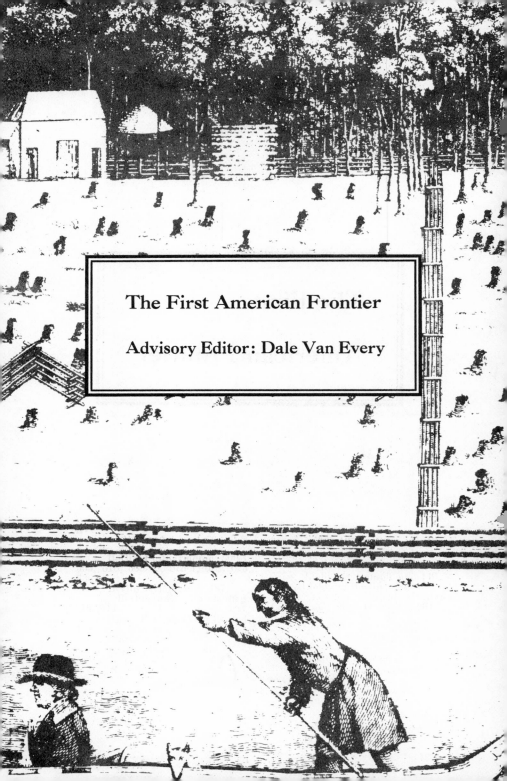

The First American Frontier

Advisory Editor: Dale Van Every

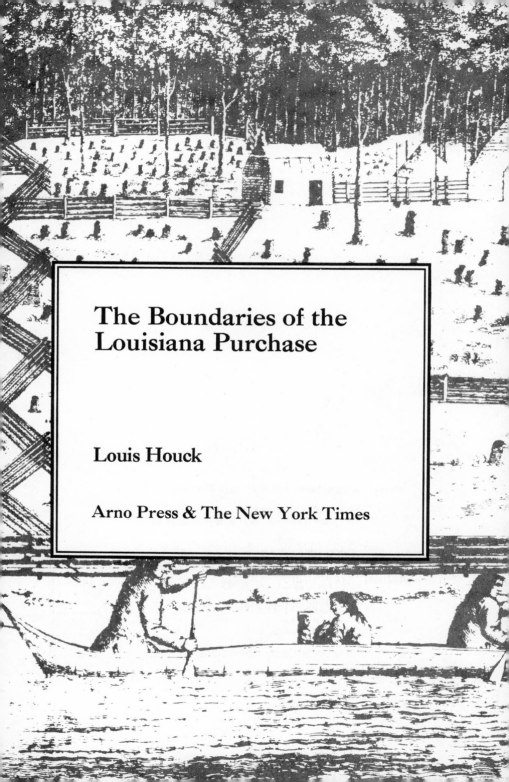

The Boundaries of the Louisiana Purchase

Louis Houck

Arno Press & The New York Times

Reprint Edition 1971 by Arno Press Inc.

Reprinted from a copy in
The State Historical Society of Wisconsin Library

LC #   72-146401
ISBN 0-405-02855-5

The First American Frontier
ISBN for complete set: 0-405-02820-2

See last pages of this volume for titles.

Manufactured in the United States of America

THE BOUNDARIES

OF THE

LOUISIANA PURCHASE

A HISTORICAL STUDY

By LOUIS HOUCK

———————

PHILLIP ROEDER'S BOOK STORE
St. Louis, Mo.

———————————

L S TAYLOR PRINTING CO - SAINT LOUIS
1901.

The fact that much erroneous infor-mation in regard to the boundaries of the Louisiana Purchase has, during the last few years, been industriously cir-culated by the daily press and otherwise, must be excuse for the publication of this study.

In the first article of the treaty of the Louisiana Purchase it is recited that "His Catholic Majesty promises and engages on his part to retrocede to the French Republic * * * the colony or province of Louisiana with the same extent that it now has in the hands of Spain, and that it had when France possessed it, and such as it should have after the treaties subsequently entered into between Spain and other states," and the First Consul of the French Republic then makes the grant in these words, i. e., "desiring to give to the United States a strong proof of his friendship, doth hereby cede to the United States in the name of the French Republic, forever and in full sovereignty, the said territory, with all its rights and appurtenances as fully and in the same manner as they had been acquired by the French Republic, in virtue of the above mentioned treaty concluded with his Catholic Majesty." No further description of the boundaries of the "colony or province of Louisiana" is given. It is transferred as the French Republic acquired it, i. e., "with the same extent that it now has in the hands of Spain and that it had when France possessed it, and such as it should be after the treaties subsequently entered into between Spain and other states." The transfer was not made by metes and bounds, because no one knew at that time the precise boundaries of the "colony or province of Louisiana." The boundaries of the colony or province were of undefined extent, so to say, political boundaries, boundaries liable to be expanded or contracted according to political exigencies.

Undeniably the purchase involved the acquisition of well defined territorial rights as well as political rights and claims. With the purchase completed we acquired that sphere of influence which France enjoyed on the North American continent by reason of the occupancy of the valley of the St. Lawrence and the Great

Lakes, and which France retained after the treaty of 1763, as well as all those territorial and political rights derived by the discovery of the Mississippi and of Texas, and which had not been ceded to Great Britain. More than that, we also acquired the territory of Louisiana "with the same extent that it now has in the hands of Spain and such as it should be after the treaties subsequently entered into between Spain and other States"— that is, when Spain retroceded the province or colony to France. In other words, if during the dominion of Spain any portion of the "colony or province of Louisiana" was lost, France re-acquired the province or colony thus curtailed. But on the other hand it is equally clear, that if during the dominion of Spain anything was added to the colony or province either territorially or politically, if vague and undefined French claims were enlarged, made certain and definite, the sphere of influence of the colony or province enlarged and broadened, thus territorially or

7

politically strengthening the colony or province, this acquisition, also inured to our benefit.

Talleyrand said: "France in giving up Louisiana to the United States trans·ferred all rights over the colony which she had acquired from Spain." (a)

In order, therefore, to determine what were the boundaries of the Louisiana Purchase, it is equally important to determine what were the boundaries territorially, and the political sphere of influence or right to expand when France ceded the colony or province to Spain, and what Spain added to or ceded away either territorially or politically pertaining to the colony or province, because as stated, if in anyway the province was curtailed or in anyway the territorial or political rights of the province enlarged and made more certain or strengthened, these rights passed to the United States.

That the United States acquired not only territorial rights, but also a sphere

(a) Letter of Talleyrand to Gen. Armstrong, Dec. 31, 1804.

8

of influence or right to expansion is shown clearly in a letter written by Mr. Livingston to Mr. Madison, Secretary of State of the United States, from Paris on May 20, 1803. In this letter Mr. Livingston says:

"I called this morning on Mr. Marbois for a further explanation of this subject (the cession of Louisiana) and to remind him of his having told me that Mobile made a part of the cession. He told me that he had no precise idea on the subject, but that he knew it to be a historical fact, and on that he had formed his opinion. I asked him what orders had been given to the Prefect, that was to take possession, or what orders had been given by Spain as to the boundary in ceding it. He assured me that he did not know, but that he would make the inquiry and let me know. At four o'clock I called for Mr. Monroe to take him to the minister for foreign affairs, but he was prevented from accompanying me. I asked the minister what were the last bounds of the territory ceded to us; he said he did not know; we must take it as they had received it; I asked him how Spain meant to give that possession; he said according to the words of the treaty; but where did you mean to take? I do not know. Then you mean that we shall construe it our own way? I can give you no direction; you have made a noble bargain for yourselves and I suppose you will make the most of it."

Hence Benton in his speech in reply to Dickerson truly said, that when the United States purchased Louisiana they acquired "with it an open question of boundaries for that vast province." (a)

When the French negotiator pointed out to Napoleon the uncertainty of the boundary he said "that if obscurity did not already exist it would perhaps be good policy to put one there." (b)

Gallatin wrote Jefferson August 18, 1803, that our minister in England, Hon. Rufus King, advised him that

(a) Benton's Thirty Years in the United States Senate, Vol. 1, p. 51.
(b) Marbois' Louisiana, p. 286.

the boundaries of Louisiana "had never been settled by any treaty." (*a*)

In 1808, "An Account of Louisiana, being an abstract of Documents in the offices of the Department of State," was published anonymously, and in this account it is said "of the province of Louisiana no general map sufficiently correct to be depended upon has been published, nor has any yet been procured from a private source. It is indeed probable that surveys have never been made on so extensive a scale as to afford the means of laying down the various regions of country which in some of it appear to have been but imperfectly explored." (*b*)

And Colonel Don Antonia de Alcedo in his "Geographical and Historical Dictionary of the West Indies of America," published by permission of the Spanish Government in Madrid in 1786, says that the "limits of the province of Louisiana have never been precisely fixed."

(*a*) Writings of Gallatin, Vol. 1, p. 143.
(*b*) Page 1.

Says McMasters, "on the rude maps of the closing days of the seventeenth century Louisiana, therefore, extends from the Rio Grande to the Mobile, from the Gulf to the country beyond the sources of the Mississippi River, from the Smoky Mountains to the unknown regions of the West." (*a*)

Du Pratz, who wrote his "History of Louisiana" before the close of the French-English wars, thus defines the boundaries: "Louisiana is that part of North America which is bounded on the south by the Gulf of Mexico, on the east by Carolina, an English colony, and by a part of Canada; on the west by New Mexico, and on the north in part by Canada, in part it extends without assignable bounds to the terra incognita adjoining Hudson Bay." (*b*)

Vague and contradictory ideas prevailed as to the boundaries of the "colony and province" because the territory was not of sufficient value or

(*a*) Hist. of the People of the United States, Vol. 3, p. 32.

(*b*) Du Pratz' Hist. of Louisana, Vol. 1, p. 200, London Edition, 1763.

well enough known to warrant a controversy, nor was it the policy of any
of the powers interested in this territory to make any concession or definite agreement as to the boundaries.

The question of the extent of the
"colony or province of Louisiana"
was left open and finally was solved
and settled by us as dictated by our
interest as a political and not as an
academic question.

The French had no idea of curtail-
ing the limits of their vast claims on
the North American continent. They
had no fixed theories about water
sheds and natural and geographical
boundaries. They claimed everything
to the "Western Sea" precisely as their
English neighbors on this continent.

The doctrine of European rights to
uncivilized countries derived from discovery and possession is not reducible
and never has been reduced to fixed
rules. (a)

French statesmen well understood
this. In 1715, Raudot, who under
Pontchartrain was in charge of French

(a) Writings of Gallatin, Vol. 1, p. 241.

colonial affairs, requested De L'Isle, the geographer, to remove the dots from his map that marked the limits of Louisiana "as the Court wishes it left undefined, and does not want French maps to be quoted by foreign nations against us." (a)

The assertion of Marbois: "The shores of the Western Ocean were certainly not comprised in the cession," (b) would have been emphatically repudiated by Pontchartrain. The statement is entitled to little consideration, because it is contradicted by the entire colonial policy and claims of France in North America.

Nor were the statesmen of our country less alive, than the statesmen of France, to save the territorial rights and to protect the sphere of political influence we secured by the acquisition of the " colony or province of Louisiana." So cautious was the United States Senate, that the fifth article of the treaty of 1803 with Great Britain for adjusting our northern

(a) Winsor's Mississippi Basin, p. 86.
(b) Marbois' Louisiana, p. 286.

boundary was rejected, because it was feared it would curtail our rights acquired from France by the Louisiana Purchase.

"It happened," says Benton, "in the very time we were signing a treaty in Paris for the acquisition of Louisiana that we were signing another in London for the adjustment of the boundary line between the Northwest possessions of the United States and the King of Great Britain. The negotiators of each were ignorant of what the other had done, and on remitting the two treaties to the Senate of the United States for ratification, that for the purchase of Louisiana was ratified without restriction; the other with the exception of the fifth article. It was this article which adjusted the boundary between the United States and Great Britain from the Lake of the Woods to the head of the Mississippi, and the Senate refused to ratify because by a possibility it might jeopardize the northern boundary of Louisiana." England rejected the treaty as amended.

If the views of the limited boundaries of the Louisiana Purchase that now are advocated by some had obtained at that time the United States would not have rejected the fifth article of the treaty, but ratified the same, and in this way a large portion of the territory that now constitutes the states of Minnesota, North Dakota and Montana undoubtedly lost to the United States.

After the sale of the "colony and province of Louisiana" to the United States the boundaries of the colony sold became a matter of indifference to France, but Spain as well as Great Britain were concerned at the time in determining what the boundaries of Louisiana were. It was the policy of both of these nations to endeavor to curtail and limit the actual territorial boundaries of the "province or colony" and the historical right of France to expand to the Western Sea, a right which we acquired by virtue of this purchase. Nothing would have better served the diplomats of Europe than the arguments advanced by some of

our writers holding quasi-governmen-
tal positions or some of the ill-con-
sidered official maps attempting to
show the extent of the Louisiana
Purchase. Such maps published in
1805 would have given England the
northwest Pacific coast and Texas to
Spain.

Without going into every detail let
us now examine what were the territorial limits of the "colony or province
of Louisiana": first, on the east;
second, on the southwest; third, on
the north; and fourth, what were the
western territorial limits and the
political sphere of influence belonging to this "colony or province", or
right of the Louisiana hinterland to
expand to the Western Ocean.

The Mississippi from the 31st degree parallel to its source was the eastern boundary of the "province or colony of Louisiana". The 31st parallel from the Mississippi to the Apalachicola, and down that stream to the Gulf, was considered by the United States, by France and England as the southeast boundary, but Spain claimed that the Iberville and Lakes Maurepas and Pontchartrain were the true dividing line between Louisiana and the Floridas. Historically, undoubtedly the boundary of the "colony or province of Louisiana" extended as far east as Pensacola. The principal seat of the colony or province was established by Iberville on the western side of the river Mobile, not far from the spot where now stands the city of Mobile, and there remained until Bienville in 1723 laid out the city of New Orleans.

Before the discovery of the mouth of the Mississippi and the voyages of

18

Iberville, the Spaniards claimed the whole circuit of the Gulf, but made no settlement—and only were aroused to action by the enterprise of the French, and then occupied the Bay of Pensacola, the best harbor on the Gulf. "The barrier thus formed," says Pickett, "made the dividing line between Florida and Louisiana." (*a*)

"All the French writers are agreed in fixing the Perdido to the east as the limits, and the Rio del Norte to the west," for Louisiana. (*b*)

In a letter to Breckenridge dated August 12th, 1803, Jefferson claims the Rio Perdido between Mobile and Pensacola as the "ancient boundary of Louisiana," and Gallatin agreed with him. (*c*)

Spain persistently for a time refused to admit the Perdido as the boundary line, and formed the territory, bounded on the north by the 31st degree, by the River Perdido on the east, the Pearl River on the west, and the Gulf of Mexico on the south, into a Spanish

(*a*) Pickett's Hist. of Alabama, Vol. 1, p. 185.
(*b*) Brackenridge's Views of Louisiana, p. 57.
(*c*) Writings of Gallatin, Vol. 1, p. 150.

district. At the same time the United States insisted that the country should be surrendered as a part of the Louisiana Purchase, and that both the Baton Rouge and Mobile districts were included in the Louisiana cession. On the other hand, it was contended by Spanish authorities that just before the Revolution she was engaged in a war with England and by conquest acquired the Baton Rouge district as well as Mobile, then being a part of West Florida, and that by the treaty of 1783 Great Britain ceded this territory to her.

For a time great excitement on account of this controversy prevailed along the borders and border troubles were the order of the day. (a)

In 1810 the Spaniards were expelled from Baton Rouge by force, the place being taken by surprise and the Spanish Governor de Grandpre was killed. After this the Spaniards of this district retired to Pensacola. In 1813 the United States became apprehensive that the British forces might

(a) Pickett's Hist. of Alabama, p. 203.

take possession of the Mobile District and forts and the whole district between the Pearl and the Perdido and below the line of the 31st degree parallel was occupied by our Government as ceded to us under the Louisiana Purchase. General Wilkinson with 600 men of the third and seventh regiments, sailing from New Orleans in transport vessels commanded by Commodore Shaw, provided with scaling ladders and every necessary equipment, landed in the Bay of Mobile, marched up to the town, took position in the rear of Fort Charlotte, and after some correspondence the Spanish Commandant, Captain Cayetano Perez, surrendered the fort, cannon and military stores to the United States, the commander of the United States forces agreeing to pay for the same, and also retired to Pensacola. The stars and stripes were hoisted on the ramparts of Fort Charlotte, and General Wilkinson then marched to the Rio Perdido and established a stockade fort there.

That the River Perdido formed the eastern boundary of Louisiana has also been decided in a number of cases by the Supreme Court of the United States. (*a*)

Thus finally by virtue of the Louisiana Purchase the southern portions of Mississippi and Alabama were added to the United States, *(b)* and to that extent Mississippi and Alabama are Louisiana Purchase States.

(*a*) See opinion of Chief Justice Marshall in Foster v. Neilson, 2 Peters, 307 affirmed in Garcia, vs. Lee, 12 Peters, page 520—Chief Justice Taney, delivering opinion of Court.

(*b*) Pickett's Hist. of Alabama, Vol. 2, p. 248.

The claim of France to Texas as a part of Louisiana was founded on the discovery of LaSalle and on the French establishments of the Mississippi being prior to those of Spain east of the Rio del Norte. (*a*)

When LaSalle established his post on Matagorda Bay, the nearest Spanish settlement was on the Panuco, and the natural half-way boundary of the unoccupied territory was the Rio Bravo. (*b*)

Bancroft says: ''Louisiana was held by the French to e x t e n d t o t h e River del Norte. The boundary line of French pretensions, in disregard of the claims of Spain, crossed the Rocky Mountains and sought its termination in the Gulf of California.'' (*c*)

Says Bancroft: ''Ascending the Lavaca, a small stream at the west of the bay, LaSalle selected a site on the

(*a*) Writings of Gallatin, Vol. 1, p. 241.
(*b*) Jefferson's letter to Mellish, Dec. 31, 1816.
(*c*) Bancroft's Hist. of the United States, Vol. 2, Chap. 14, p. 214, Author's last revision,

open ground for the establishment of a fortified post. The gentle slope which he named St. Louis showed towards the west and southwest a boundless landscape, verdant with luxuriant grasses and dotted with groves of forest trees; south and east was the Bay of Matagorda skirted with prairies. The waters which abounded in fish attracted flocks of wild fowl; the fields were alive with deer and bison and wild turkeys, and the deadly rattle-snake, bright inhabitant of the meadows. There under the suns of June with timber felled in an inland grove and dragged for a league over the prairie grass the colonists prepared to build a shelter, LaSalle being the architect and himself marking the beams, the tenons and mortises. With parts of t h e w r e c k brought up on canoes a second house was framed, and of each the roof was covered with buffalo skins. Thus France took possession of Texas; her arms carved on its trees, and by no

24

treaty or public document or map did she give up her right to the province until she resigned the whole of Louisiana to Spain.'' (a)

LaHarpe made a second attempt to plant a colony on the Bay of Matagorda, but this stimulated the Spaniards to the occupation of the country by the establishments from time to time of several forts.

The French ever regarded the mouth of del Norte as the western limit of Louisiana on the Gulf of Mexico. An English geography (Poples' map) recognized the claim.

When in 1819 Don Louis de Onis was commissioned by Spain to settle the boundary dispute of Louisiana, the United States contended that Texas was a part of Louisiana, and the contention was based on the discovery of the Mississippi throughout its whole length in 1682 by LaSalle; the landing of LaSalle in Matagorda Bay in 1685; the grant of Louis XIV. to Crozat; a memoir said to have been

(a) Bancroft's Hist. of the United States, Vol. 2, p. 172, Author's last revision.

written by Vergennes in the reign of Louis XVI.; a chart of Louisiana by Lopez publishsd in 1762; a map of DeL'Isle published in 1782; a map published at Nurenburg in 1712; an "Atlas Geographicus" published in London in 1717; an official British map published in 1755; Narratives of Hennepin, Tonty and Joutel; letter of LaHarpe dated July 8, 1719; an order from Bienville to LaHarpe d a t e d August 12, 1771; and the geographical work of Alcedo, already referred to, published in Spain. (*a*)

Falconer attempts to throw discredit on this formidable array of authorities by claiming that they are mostly irrelevent, the maps unofficial, and that both the map-makers of London and Nurenberg must be put out of Court; but it should be remembered that he is arguing the British side in this controversy as to the Louisiana boundary. On an array of authorities far less decisive and clear Great Britain secured great and important territories.

(*a*) See Falconer on the Mississippi and Oregon, p. 41, and where authorities are set out as above.

How active the French were in asserting claim to Texas as a part of Louisiana is shown by the fact that Iberville sent out exploring parties westward feeble as the French colonies were. In 1716 Cadillac sent St. Dennis to oppose the Spaniards in an attempt to establish themselves at Nachitoches. (a)

In 1718 St. Dennis with another expedition penetrated as far south as the Presidio of St. John the Baptist on the Rio del Norte. A French fort was established at Nachitoches in 1730, St. Dennis acting as commandant. (b) In 1720 LaHarpe built a fort in latitude 35, 55, about 250 miles from Nachitoches, which he called St. Louis del Carlorette, and the French remained in possession until the country was transferred to Spain. (c) From this fort LaHarpe explored the country to the Arkansas, examined the sources of the Washita, passed the high moun-

(a) Gayarres' Hist. of Louisiana, p. 166.

(b) Gayarres' Hist. of Louisiana, p. 418: Du Pratz, Vol. 1, p. 11.

(c) Brackenridge's Views of Louisiana, p. 56.

tains, which divided the waters of the Washita from the Arkansas, and descended that river to the Mississippi. (a)

It must, however, not be supposed that the Spaniards were idle. They also established forts and posts, notably San Antonio de Bexar. The Spanish Governor ordered LaHarpe to retire from Texas, but LaHarpe replied that he was astonished at the pretensions of the Spanish Governor, considering that the French had always looked upon Texas as a part of Louisiana, since LaSalle had taken possession of that country, and which still retained his mortal remains. He added that the French Government could not admit that the pretensions of Spain could legitimately go beyond the Rio Bravo. The French Government supported LaHarpe in the position he had taken, and he was ordered to take possession of the Bay of St. Bernard.

Gayarre says: ''It is not the less remembered that France called in

(a)   Brackenridge's Views of Louisiana, p. 58.

question rights which Spain pretended with so much tenacity to have to Texas. (*a*)

Although the claims of the United States were abandoned by the Florida treaty signed at Washington on the 22nd day of February, 1819, this in no wise ought to be taken as evidence that Texas was not truly a part of the "colony or province of Louisiana". It should rather be considered as dictated by the exigencies of the hour. Says President Monroe: "For the territory ceded by Spain other territory of great value (Texas to which our claim was believed to be well founded) was ceded by the United States, and in a quarter more interesting to her." (*b*)

But Jefferson was inflexibly opposed to this treaty. (*c*) So also Jackson, but he yielded to the arguments of Monroe, and wrote that "for the present we ought to be contented with the Floridas." (*d*) Benton was

(*a*) Hist. of Louisiana, p. 260; See also Falconer, p. 41.

(*b*) Message of President Monroe, Dec. 7, 1819.

(*c*) Benton's Thirty Years, Vol. 1, p. 16.

(*d*) See Benton's Thirty Years, Vol. 1, p. 16.

"shocked" by this treaty, because the new boundary, "besides cutting off Louisiana, dismembered the valley of the Mississippi, mutilated two of its noblest rivers, brought foreign dominion (and it non-slave holding) to the neighborhood of New Orleans, and established a wilderness barrier between Missouri and New Mexico to interrupt their trade, separate their inhabitants and shelter the wild Indian depredators upon the lives and property of all who undertook to pass from one to the other." (a)

Chevalier de Onis claimed the praise of his nation for having exchanged the small and comparatively unimportant province of Florida for the rich and productive territory of Texas, thus admitting that Texas constituted truly a part of the Louisiana Purchase. But Falconer says that Chevalier de Onis did not manage the case of Spain well, and that "a more gross case of mismanagement and ignorant diplomacy was never exhibited."

(a) Benton's Thirty Years, Vol. 1, p. 15.

By this treaty Spain ceded Florida and the United States relinquished all claims to territories west of the River Sabine and south of the upper parts of the Red and Arkansas rivers. It was agreed that a line drawn on the meridian from the source of the Arkansas northward to the 42nd parallel of latitude, thence along that parallel westward to the Pacific should form the northern boundary of the Spanish possessions and the southern boundary of those of the United States in that quarter—"His Catholic Majesty ceding to the United States all his rights, claims, and pretensions to any territories north of said line". This line fixed definitely the south line of the L o u i s i a n a Purchase to the Pacific. (*a*)

Although Texas was thus ceded away, subsequent events restored this portion of the "colony or province of Louisiana" to the United States, (*b*) and hence it seems proper that Texas should be considered as one of the Louisiana Purchase states.

(*a*) Greenhow's, p. 316.

(*b*) See President Tyler's message to the Senate, 1844, Messages and Papers of the Presidents, Vol. 4, p. 307.

The northern limits of Louisiana were never definitely determin- ed. (a) In 1717 the Illinois country was added to Louisiana, but it was uncertain whether this carried the line to the Wisconsin River, and it was a source of dispute between Vaudreuil, Governor of Canada, and Boisbriant, Local Governor of Ft. de Chartres, whether his jurisdiction ex- tended to the source of all the affluents of the Mississippi or not. (b) Some map makers included the basin of Lake Winipeg as in the Louisiana country. Hennepin's map of Louisiana extends the boundaries of Louisiana north of Lake Superior. (c)

According to Du Pratz Louisiana on the north in part extends without any assignable bounds to the terraincog- nita adjoining to the Hudson's Bay. (d)

(a) Winsor's Miss. Basin, p. 146.
(b) Winsor's Miss. Basin, p. 148.
(c) See map in Winsor's Cartier to Frontenac, p. 279.
(d) Du Pratz Hist. of Louisiana, Vol. 1, p. 199.

"However, "he says," we need not trouble ourselves concerning our interests in this very distant region. Many centuries must pass before we shall have penetrated these northern countries of Louisiana."

But as the northern boundary of the "colony or province of Louisiana" the United States claimed the 49th parallel of latitude upon the ground that this parallel had been adopted and definitely settled by commissioners appointed agreeably to the 10th article of the Peace of Utrecht in 1713. Says Gallatin: "The limits between the possessions of Great Britain and those of ours in the same quarter, namely, Canada and Louisiana, were determined by commissioners appointed in pursuance of the treaty of Utrecht. From the coast of Labrador to a certain point north of Lake Superior those limits were fixed according to certain metes and bounds, and from that point the line of demarcation was agreed to extend indefinitely west along the 49th parallel north latitude. It was in conformity with that arrangement that the United States claimed that parallel as the northern boundary of Louisiana. It has been accordingly thus settled as far as the Stony Mountains by the convention of 1818, between the United States and Great Britain, and no adequate reason can be given why the same boundary should not be continued as far as the claims of the United States extend—that is to say, as far as the Pacific Ocean.'' (a)

But Greenhow makes it quite clear that these commissioners never did definitely agree upon this boundary line. (b)

Universally, however, the 49th parallel came to be considered, in this country, as the boundary line established under that treaty; but on some maps the highlands encircling Hudson Bay were laid down as the boundary line under the treaty of Utrecht, and on other maps, published by authority of the British Government, no line was laid down at all; and, according to Pere Marest, the French in 1694,

(a) Writings of Gallatin, Vol. 3, p. 310.
(b) See Greenhow's Oregon, p. 281.

before this treaty was made and which merely confirmed English rights, claimed the right to trade in the Hudson Bay country "to the 51st degree parallel and even further north." (a)

By the treaty of 1873 it was agreed between Great Britain and the United States that our northern boundary line should pass "through Lake Superior northward to the isles Royal and Philipeaux to the Long Lake, thence through the middle of the Long Lake, between it to the Lake of the Woods; thence through the said lake to the northwestern point thereof, and from thence on a due west course to the River Mississippi; thence by a line drawn along the middle of said River Mississippi until it shall intersect the northermost part of the 31st degree north latitude."

When this northern line was adopted it was supposed that the 49th parallel crossed the Mississippi somewhere, but it was afterwards found that the highest water of this river did not extend beyond latitude 47 degrees, 36

(a) 66 Jesuits' Relations, p. 69.

minutes north, and that the northern point of the Lake of the Woods stood in latitude 49 degrees 20 minutes north, or about 104 geographical miles north of the sources of the Mississippi.

An effort was made in 1794 to make an amicable adjustment of this anomly, but nothing definite resulted. By the treaty of 1803 already referred to it was agreed that the northern boundary between Great Britian and the United States should be from the Lake of the Woods to the Mississippi by the shortest line, but the purchase of the ''colony or province of Louisiana'' gave a new importance to this subject, and the treaty was not ratified.

By the treaty of 1807, it was attempted to fix the 49th parallel as the boundary between the United States and Great Britain as far as the Rocky Mountains, but this treaty was also rejected, because the line along the 49th parallel was not extended westward to the Pacific Ocean.

Thus early was the 49th parallel claimed and recognized as our northern boundary by virtue of the Louisiana Purchase and admitted to be the line of the Louisiana Purchase as far as the Rocky Mountains by Great Britain, and thus a large portion of the territory now lying in the states of Minnesota, North Dakota and Montana secured.

According to the treaty of 1783 our limits did not extend beyond the headwaters of the Mississippi a s stated, being 47 degrees and 30 minutes north parallel, and Falconer says that ''nothing west or north of this line (that is, a line from the head of the Lake of the Woods as set out in the treaty of 1783 to the headwaters of the Mississippi) was granted by Great Britain to the United States in 1783, and nothing north of the headwaters of the Mississippi was retained by France under the treaty of 1763''. (a)

What we acquired north of the 47th degree 30 minutes parallel and west of a line drawn from the head of the Lake of the Woods and the Mississippi we owe entirely to the purchase

(a) On the Mississippi and Oregon, p. 36.

of the "colony and province of Louisiana" and the uncertainty of the northern boundary thus acquired.

In those early negotiations Great Britain set up no claim to the territory south of the 49th parallel and west of the Rocky Mountains, but different efforts were made "to overreach the Americans with respect to the country west of the Rocky Mountains." And without presenting any claim "they endeavored to leave a nest-egg for future pretentions in that quarter." (a) At that time no American publisher or map-maker was engaged in furnishing arguments to advance British pretensions.

(a)   State Papers 1822-3 cited in Benton's Thirty Years. Vol. 1, p. 51.

The boundaries on the west of "the vast, ill-defined region known as Louisiana," (*a*) according to Stoddard, ran from "a remarkable bend" in the Rio Bravo "about 29 degrees, 25 minutes, north latitude, near which is the southern extremity of the Mexican Mountains," and which was the line of demarcation between Louisiana and the Spanish possessions, and there "leaves the river, diverges a little to the right, and runs along to the northwest on the summit of these mountains till it terminates in the 46th degree of north latitude" (*b*). But Franquelins map of 1684 does not carry the mountains further north than the 40th degree, and nothing north of the 40th degree parallel by this map is admitted to belong to Spain. On this map "la Grande Riviere des Emissourites" is shown as far north as the 38 degree north parallel. On the other hand, the map

(*a*) Roosevelt's Winning the West, Vol. 1, p. 19.
(*b*) Stoddard's Louisiana, p. 146,

published with Charlevoix' History
of New France "Dressee par N. B.
Ing du Roy, et Hydrg de la Marine,"
dated 1743, clearly marks an advance
of geographical knowledge, as well as
an advance of the French claims on
this continent. The New Mexican
Mountains are shown to extend north
to the 42nd or 43rd degree parallel,
but beyond the words "Nouvelle
France" are carried across the continent from the Mer de l'Ouest to the
Atlantic. The territory south of "St.
Fez" is designated as "Nouveau Mex-
ique." The Missouri seems to be
laid down so as to head off the Mexican Mountains extending north of the
Rio Bravo to about the 43rd parallel.
Certainly these two maps do not show
that the Spanish pretensions extend
as far as the "46th degree north latitude." The map attached to the
History of Louisiana by du Pratz, and
to which Stoddard makes reference,
seems to carry the Spanish boundaries
no farther than the 41st degree north
latitude, (a) and the dotted lines on

(a) See map dated 1757 attached to the History of
Louisiana by du Pratz, London Edition, 1763.

this map especially show an attempt
to mark the boundary line between
the French and Spanish possessions
on the west and north.

The Spaniards seemed little in-
clined to extend their claim further
eastward than the summit of the
so - called Mexican Mountains. It
is true that in 1720 they sent an
expedition to the Missouri, attempting to make an establishment on
that river, but the Indians utterly
destroyed the entire party, and after
that no Spanish efforts were made to
interfere with the French pretensions.
(*a*) For over eighty years the French
controlled, to their sources, all the
rivers emptying into the Mississippi
from the west, and "hence the proba-
bility is strong that they (the Spaniards) considered the Mexican Mountains, or sources of the rivers in them,
as the western limits of Louisiana"
(*b*) as far north as the mountains ran,
or were known; namely, to about the
42nd or 43rd degree north latitude.

(*a*) See Bossu's Travels, Vol. 1, p. 151.
(*b*) Stoddard's Louisiana, p. 134.

41

It should not be forgotten that the Colorado, Trinity, Red River, Arkansas, Platte and some other large rivers have their springs in these mountains. (*a*) That the Spaniards considered these mountains as the limit dividing their possessions from those of the French is also shown by the fact that when some French traders made a temporary establishment in these mountains for the purpose of trade, and were imprisoned at the instance of the Santa Fe merchants, because they deemed this French trading establishment an infringement of their rights, they were ultimately liberated and their goods restored to them by a decision of the superior court at "the Havannah" on the ground that the French establishment was located on the west side of the summit of the Mexican Mountains. (*b*) But by the treaty of 1819 the United States relinquished to Spain the district of country west of the Sabine and south of the upper part of the Red and Arkansas Rivers, and a line drawn on

(*a*)   Stoddard's Louisiana, p. 146.
(*b*)   See Stoddard's Louisiana, p. 146.

the meridian from the source of the Arkansas north to the 42nd parallel of latitude was definitely made the western boundary of Louisiana and the 42nd degree north parallel, extending to the Pacific Ocean, was also fixed as the northern limit of the Spanish possessions, this being about the line indicated on the French maps as the utmost northern limit of the Spanish pretenisons. (a)

The western boundary of the "province or colony of Louisiana" north of the 42nd parallel has, however, given rise to great controversy.

In the "Account of Louisiana" already referred to it is said that "the precise boundaries of Louisiana westwardly of the Mississippi, though very extensive, are at present enveloped in some obscurity." (b) No discoveries

(a) "Before we conclude, it may be of use to remark that the Shining Mountains and the Mexican Mountains, though often confounded, are, in a great measure, distinct. The former are the Andes of South America; the latter commence some distance to the northward of the Gulf and run to the left of the bank of the Rio Bravo, and extend, in a northerly direction, a little to the eastward of Santa Fe until they intersect the former. They are probably branches or spurs of the Shining Mountains." (Stoddard's Louisiana, p. 149.)

(b) Page 1.

on the Missouri beyond the Mandans were accurately detailed, "though the traders have been informed that many large navigable waters discharge their waters into it far above it, and that there are many numerous nations settled on them." (a)

"The extent of Louisiana," it is said in the secret instructions to General Victor, "is well determined on the south by the Gulf of Mexico, but bounded on the west by the river called Bravo, from its mouth to about the 30th degree parallel. The line of demarcation stops on reaching this point, and there seems never to have been any agreement in regard to this part of the frontier. The further we go northward, the more undecided the boundary. This part of North America contains little more than uninhabited forests or Indian tribes, and the necessity of fixing a boundary has never yet been felt there. There also exists none between Louisiana and Canada." (b)

(a) Page 28.
(b) Secret Instructions of Decres to General Victor. Archives de la Marine, MMS. cited in Henry Adams' History of U. S., 3rd Vol., p. 32.

And in a memorial prepared in Paris in 1718, cited by Winsor, and in which is outlined a plan to give Louisiana a dominating position in North America, it was urged that one branch of the Missouri led to the South Sea, and that on that route a trade could be opened with China and Japan, thus showing that at that time the French claim extended to the Pacific Ocean. (a)

As early as 1720 it was conjectured that west of the headwaters of the Missouri a great river flowed westward, and Coxe in his Carolana makes one of the branches of this western stream interlock with the branches of the Missouri. (b)

The uncertainty of the boundaries of Louisiana in this quarter did not result from any uncertainty as to the claims made by France in North America. France always claimed the Western Ocean as the boundary of her American possessions. As early

(a) Winsor's Miss. Basin, p. 112.

(b) Winsor's Miss. Basin. p. 138 and 217. Also see Historical Collection of Louisiana, by French, Vol. 2, page 230, where Coxe's work is given in full.

as June 14th, 1671, de St. Lusson at a great gathering of all the Indian tribes held at Sault St. Marys "in the name of the most High, most Mighty and most Redoubtable Monarch, Louis XIV. of the name, the most Christian King of France and Navarre," took possession of all the "countries, rivers, lakes and tributaries contiguous and adjacent thereunto as well discovered as to be discovered, which are bounded on the one side by the Northern and Western seas and on the other side by the South sea, including all its length and breadth." (a)

And l'Escarbot, in his History of New France, written in 1687, thus describes its limits: "Our Canada has for its limits on the west side the lands as far as the sea called the Pacific on this side of the Tropic of Cancer." (b)

DuLuth intended in 1680 to push an expedition westward to the Salt Water, which he supposed to be the Gulf of California and only twenty days' journey distant. (c)

(a)   11th Wisconsin Hist. Col., p. 28.
(b)   Cited in Brower's Miss. River and its Sources,
Minn. Hist, Col., Vol. 7, p. 97, note.
(c)   Winsor's Cartier to Frontenac, p. 274.

In 1720 the celebrated Pere Charlevoix was expressly commissioned by
the French Government to visit Canada to seek a route to the Western sea.
In the Journal of the Jesuits for the
year 1720, under the date of August
7th, his arrival is thus chronicled:
"La Pere Charlevoix arrived from
France by order of the Court to col-
lect information for the discovery of
the Mer d'Occident. He is to re-
turn by Mobile." (a)

For many years it was the dream of
the French Jesuits and explorers to
find the "Sea of China" by a river
discharging its waters into the Vermil-
lion sea or Gulf of California.

After Marquette discovered from the
direction of the Mississippi, that it
probably discharged its waters into the
Gulf of Mexico, he says that he hopes
by means of the Pekitanoui (Missouri),
according to the reports made to him
by the savages, "to find it leading towards California." From the savages
he writes: "I have learned that by
ascending this river, (the Missouri)

(a)   59 Jesuits Relations, p. 235.

for five or six days one reaches a fine prairie twenty or thirty leagues long. This must be crossed in a northwest-ernly direction, and it terminates at another small river on which one may embark, for it is not difficult to trans-fer canoes in so fine a country as that prairie. This second river flows to-wards the Southwest for ten or fifteen leagues, after which it enters a lake small and deep, which flows towards the West, where it falls into the sea, and I do not despair of discovering it some day, if God grant me the cross and health to do so, in order that I may preach the gospel to this new world, which has so long grovelled in the darkness of infidelity." (a)

And LaHontan in speaking of his pretended journey in 1688 up the "Long River," supposed to be the Missouri, and on which LaHontan may or may not have traveled, first mentions the Rocky Mountains, and then says that on a deer skin map the Indians laid down a river flowing westward. "All they could say," he

(a) 59 Jesuits's Relations, p. 143.

writes, "was that the Great River of that nation runs all along westward, and that the Salt Lake into which it falls is 300 leagues in circumference and thirty in breadth, its mouth stretching a great way to the Southward." LaHontan usually is altogether discredited and deemed unworthy of belief, but information to some extent correct he certainly obtained, and some of his statements have been confirmed by subsequent discoveries. In reporting and taking for true the fabulous tales of some of his Indian informants, and reporting them without discrimination he followed the foot-steps of many of the early American travelers and chroniclers. It is said that LaHontan was a free thinker and a free writer, and that therefore his work and writings were traduced and discredited. (a) And this may be the reason why a learned priest named Babe denounced the pretended claim of La Houtan of a journey up the "Long River."

(a) H. H. Bancroft's Hist. of the N. W., Vol. 1, p. 889.

But Babe in 1716 wrote to De L'Isle, Geographer of Sciences in Paris, that towards the sources of the Mississippi "there is a highland that leads to the Western Ocean," and it is said he greatly tormented the Governor-General of Canada, M. Raudot and M. Duche "to endeavor to discover this ocean."

In 1731, Sieur de la Verendrye (*a*) endeavored to establish a chain of forts and posts across the continent as far as the South Sea. He gradually erected his forts, trading and trafficing westward. In 1738 he built Fort La Reine, in 1742 reached the Yellow Stone. On the first of January, 1743, his eldest son Pierre, accompanied by his brother and two Frenchmen, discovered and faced the craggy and snow-clad Rocky Mountains, made the ascent near the present site of Helena and took possession of the valley of the Missouri for France. (*b*)

And speaking of la Verendrye, Pere Nau says in his letter dated Oct.

(*a*) The name of Verendrye according to Sulte, spelled fourteen different ways in different documents.

(*b*) H. H. Bancroft's Hist. of Montana, p. 600.

2, 1735. "I had a pretty long conversation with la Verendrye, who is in command of the three most western forts. I understood from the interview that not much reliance can be placed on what he says concerning white-bearded savages. The Western Sea would have been discovered long ago if people had wished it. Monsieur de Count de Maurepas is right when he says that "the officials in Canada are looking not for the Western Sea, but for the Sea of Beaver." (a)

As early as 1724 M. DuBourgmont made extensive explorations northwest from Fort Orleans, located near the mouth of the Osage, going up the Missouri River accompanied by a few French soldiers and a large party of friendly Indians.

In no wise did the work of exploration relax. On the contrary the claim of France to the Western Ocean as the boundary of her American possessions was always asserted, and constant efforts were made to discover the path that would lead to that ocean.

(a)   68 Jesuits' Relations, p. 283.

A map accompanying Charlevoix' History, published in 1743, shows Mer de L'Ouest as the western boundary of New France. (*a*) This map also shows that the "River of the West" is laid down south of the 50th parallel to ''Ice suivant le raport des Sauvages commence la Flux et reflux''

In 1758, in his History of Louisiana (*b*), M. La Page du Pratz gives an account of the discovery of the Western Sea by Moncachtape, a Yazoo Indian living among the Natchez, and who was known to the French as l'Interpret, because master of many languages. Moncachtape was a most remarkable man, possessed of a remarkable mind and of an eager thirst for knowledge. In about the year 1745, so du Pratz relates, he crossed the Mississippi to explore the country along the sources of the Missouri. He spent a winter with the Missouris, learned the language of the Kansas Indians residing further up the river,

(*a*) See copy of map Shea's Translation of Charlevoix' History of New France.
(*b*) Vol. 2, p. 120, edition of 1763, London.

then in a pirogue began to ascend the Great River, and undismayed by the tales of peril, finally reached the snow-clad Rocky Mountains. While hesitating whether to proceed, he saw a smoke arise, and supposing that it came from a camp, he found, to his joy, that he was not mistaken and that some thirty men and women of the Otter nation were moving eastward buffalo hunting. He did not understand their language, but made himself understood by signs. With one of those Indians returning west as a guide, Moncachtape passed over the worst part of the rocky route. For nine short days he still further ascended the waters of the Missouri, then marched north for five days, and at the end of this time reached a clean and beautiful water called, for this reason, the Beautiful River, and following this river with his guide, arrived at the village of the Otter tribe. Here our Indian explorer remained for a fortnight to learn some of the language, then departing he floated down the river for eighteen days,

where he remained at another village
with a friendly Indian tribe, in order
to learn more of the language, further
down the stream, so that he would
be able to understand all the nations
which he might find on his way to
the Great Water. Finally he departed
from this village, and, after many
incidents, reached a people residing
then one day's journey from the ocean,
and, after various adventures, he jour-
neyed along the coast still farther
north until he ascertained that all was
a cold, barren and desolate waste,
then he turned his face homeward,
where he arrived after an absence of
five years. Here du Pratz met him,
questioned him closely, and finally
records his journey, giving it as his
opinion that he had found the Western
Sea, so much discussed in Louisiana,
and which all were so desirous to
discover, and there is no reason to
doubt it—the mountains, the river and
the sea are there to-day, as Moncachtape described them, and let it be
remembered, no other person, white
or red, so far as known, had ever be-

fore performed this journey between the Mississippi and the Pacific Ocean by way of the Columbia River. (*a*)

In his map of Louisiana published in 1757 du Pratz shows the route of Moncachtape and the Belle River flowing from the Rocky Mountains westward. So that at that time undoubtedly the headwaters of the Columbia were to some extent known and claimed to belong to Louisiana. Charlevoix also came to to the conclusion "in a general way that the Missouri somewhere in its springs did interlock with other waters which sought towards the west an unknown sea." (*b*)

It is certain that Jefferson was familiar with the narrative of du Pratz of the journey of Moncachtape, as would appear from his letter of instruction to Lewis, as well as with Charlevoix's views and maps.

Bougainville, Chief of Staff of Montcalm, in a memoir on the State of Canada, published in 1757, gives and account of the posts west of

(*a*) H. H. Bancroft's History of the N. W., Vol. 1, p. 607.

(*b*) Winsor's Miss. Basin, p. 138.

Lake Superior and says: "La Mer d'Ouest *is a post* that includes the Forts St. Pierre, St. Charles, Bourbon, de la Reine, Dauphine, Paskoyas and des Prairies—all of which are built with palisades that could give protection only against the Indians."

Although under this name the post of "the Sea of the West" was embraced, according to Bougainville, the whole country from Rainy Lake to the Rocky Mountains and from North Saskatchewan to the Missouri, and the Sea was not mentioned as boundary, the fact that all the forts embraced within this enormous district were designated "as a post" named "La Mer d'Ouest," (*a*) significantly points to the fact that the Sea of the West was considered the western boundary.

Marbois says: "According to old documents the Bishopric of Louisiana extended to the Pacific Ocean, and the limits of the dioceses thus defind were secure from all dispute. But this was at most a matter of expectancy, and the Indians of these regions never had

(*a*) Warren's Hist. of the Ojibways, p. 426.

any suspicion of the spiritual jurisdiction which it was designed to ex-
ercise over them. Besides it had no
connection with the rights of sovereignty of property.'' (*a*) No one must
have known better than Marbois that
the fact that the Bishopric of Louisiana was extended as far as the Pacific
Ocean was based on the idea that the
territory was French territory and the
expectation that the civil jurisdiction
of the French Government would be
extended so as to include the limits
so described. It is true the country
was unexplored, but it was certainly
claimed to be within the French sphere
of discovery. Possessed of the Rocky
Mountain hinterland and the headwaters of the Columbia, France natur-
ally would claim the control of the
Columbia to its mouth, and to the
ocean, just as France claimed possession of the mouth of the Mississippi
by virtue of discovering the headwaters
of this stream and following its waters
to the Gulf of Mexico, although prior
to the discovery and exploration of the

(*a*) Marbois Louisiana, p. 284.

Mississippi by France Spanish explorers had crossed and re-crossed the stream at various times, and although Spain claimed exclusive control of the whole coast of the Gulf of Mexico, and the Gulf itself was considered a Spanish inland sea.

So also when France ceded to Great Britain her claim to the Hudson Bay country the claim was expanded to the Northern Ocean and westwardly to the Pacific Ocean from her settlements on that bay. (a)

After the province of Louisiana passed into the hands of Spain the work of exploration did not cease. The limits of geographical and topographical knowledge of the great interior of the continent were constantly extended and enlarged, but in accordance with the well known and illiberal policy of Spain, no publication, or at most meagre publications of the discoveries and labors of the Spanish discoverers were made. Their reports were buried in the Spanish archives, and often the explorers and voyagers

(a) Calhoun's Works, Vol. 5, p. 454.

of other nations reaped the glory and reward more justly due the Spaniards by right of priority.

During the Spanish dominion of Louisiana, frequent expeditions were made up the Missouri and to the headwaters of the Columbia.

That the Spanish authorities were actively at work to enlarge the limits of human knowledge and to carry explorations beyond the sources of the Missouri, expecting thus to discover the Pacific, claiming all the intermediate country as within "the province and colony of Louisiana" is clearly shown by a petition addressed to Don Manual Gayoso de Lemos, Governor-General of the Province of Louisiana, by one Joseph Robideaux, Indian trader in St. Louis, setting forth his grievances against Claymorgan, and in which he alleges that on May 12, 1794, Don Zenon Trudeau, Lieutenant-Governor of the western part of Illinois, called the traders together to unite in a co-partnership, consolidate their respective capitals to control the trade in peltries then carried on in the upper Missouri, explaining to them at the same time that it was his purpose "to enlighten the age in regard to that portion of the globe, as yet so little known," and that to this purpose "he required that in pursuing this trade those engaged in it would pay attention to unite to the employees they might send to the country, enlightened persons, and use every exertion to penetrate the sources of the Missouri, and beyond, if possible, to the Southern Ocean," and to acquire a correct knowledge of the country till then almost entirely unknown. (a)

And in another petition, dated March 1st, 1797, Don Jaque Claymorgan claims that he was employed by the Spanish Government to explore the Indian nations as far as the Pacific Ocean, and that in order to defray the excessive expenses and at the same time to keep off the foreign traders of Hudson Bay and Lake Superior, an annual allowance of ten thousand dollars was made by the Spanish Government. The Spanish company, of

(a) Billon's Annals of St. Louis, Vol. 1, p. 281.

which Claymorgan was the leading spirit, was organized in 1794, in St. Louis, as stated in his petition by Robideaux, with the object to engage in the fur trade on the upper Missouri, and by a special royal order, dated May 27, 1792, the organization of the company was approved, and it was authorized to maintain a hundred armed men in its forts at royal expense. The money, however, stipulated to be paid these soldiers in the forts, was never paid. A land grant was afterwards made to Claymorgan, and in supporting his land grant he refers to his services as an explorer and the usual method of payment by grants of land under the Spanish Government. Stoddard says: "The Spanish Government never gave any salaries to its provincial officers, nor any gratuities in money, to those who, amid dangers and at great expense, explored unknown regions and made new discoveries, but when compensations were solicited, it was usual to to bestow tracts of land instead of money." (*a*) Accordingly, a large

(*a*) Sketches of Louisiana, p. 257.

grant of many thousand acres of land was granted by Lieutenant-Governor Zenon Trudeau to Claymorgan, and in an argument, after the acquisition of Louisiana, to secure a confirmation of this claim by Congress, it was claimed and asserted that he crossed the Rocky Mountains and reached the Pacific. His representatives said ''to explore the sources of the Missouri and to arrive at the South Sea by crossing the Shining Mountains, was a project honorable to those who performed it and interesting to the human race. It was a scheme of discovery calculated to enlarge the boundaries of human knowledge, to open new sources of national wealth, to carry the light of civilization to many unlettered barbarians, and in time to revive, upon the Western coast of America, the fame of the ancient cities which rose successfully upon the different channels of Eastern commerce and fell with its loss. It was an enterprise full of peril, of difficulty and of glory. It was conceived under the enlightened administration of the Governor-General of Louisiana, the Baron de Carondelet, and was executed under the patronage of our own immortal Jefferson. The names of Lewis and Clark live under the recollections of this grand event. Their precursor in the path of peril, but not in renown, was Don Jaque Claymorgan. He was the chosen instrument of Baron de Carondelet. He embarked his fortune to make discoveries, to found a commercial company, to conciliate barbarians, to make head against British influence and to make for his king the advantage he had by the establishments of forts and garrisons." (a)

Among others James McKay was also authorized to make a voyage of discovery up the Missouri to last for six years by Carondelet. He was identified with the Claymorgan Commercial Company and secured a land grant for his alleged services, but how far northwest he went or what discoveries he made has not been recorded.

(a) American State Papers, Pub. Lands, Vol. 3, p. 270.

Also a map said to have been accurate of the Missouri River was made by a Mr. Evans for the Spanish Government as far as the Mandans, and this map was afterwards transmitted by Jefferson to Lewis to aid him on his voyage of exploration. (a)

While thus from the interior explorations were made of the upper portion of the Missouri Basin and the headwaters of the Columbia, the Spaniards were not idle on the Pacific coast. Leaving out of view the early voyages along the northwest coast, it is undoubtedly true that the whole extent of the northwest coast territory was formal taken possession of by Juan Perez in 1773, and that he carefully examined the whole littoral.

In 1775 a second expedition under Bruno de Heceta was sent out, consisting of four vessels, and on June 13th, in latitude 47 degrees and 30 minutes Europeans first set foot on the soil of the coast. Capt. Heceta and a few sailors landed in the morning, erected a cross and took actual

(a) Lewis and Clerk's Expedition, Vol. 1 p. XXXII (Coues' Edition.)

possession. Sailing along the coast on the 17th of August Hecata in the afternoon discovered a bay with a strong current and eddies, indicating the mouth of a great river or strait in latitude 46 degrees and 9 minutes, and which he named Bahia de la Asuncion, calling the northern point San Roque, and the southern Cabo Frondoso, this being what is now called the mouth of the Columbia River, between Capes Disappointment and Adams. No further explorations were attemped. The reports of these expeditions were not published, and by this mistaken policy the Spanish navigators lost most of the honor due them. (a)

So that if any doubt existed as to whether Louisiana extended to the Western Sea these discoveries and this formal occupation of the country would seem to have undoubtedly perfected the title of Spain to this part of Louisiana.

Jefferson even before the treaty of cession in a message to Congress in 1803 suggested an expedition up the

(a) H. H. Bancroft's Hist. of the N. W., Vol. 1, p 158, et seq.

Missouri to secure the trade of the Indian tribes residing along that river, and "offering, according to best accounts, a continued navigation from its sources, and possibly with a single portage from the Western Ocean," and he thought that "an intelligent officer with ten or twelve chosen men, fit for the enterprise" might "explore the whole line even to the Western Ocean, have conferences with the natives on subjects of commercial intercourse, get admission among them for our traders as others are admitted," etc., and requested from Congress an appropriation of $2500 for the purpose of extending the external commerce of the United States.

From his letter of instructions to Lewis, dated, June 13, 1803, it is evident that Jefferson thought the Louisiana Purchase extended to the Pacific Ocean, although in a letter dated August 12, 1803, addressed to Mr. Breckenridge he says: "The boundary which I deem not admitting question of are the highlands on the western side of the Mississippi, enclosing

all its waters, the Missouri, of course."
To that extent it is to be inferred from
this letter he considered the boundary
as being undoubted. As to how far
further west the boundary might or
could extend was evidently an open
question with him.

In another letter addressed to Lewis
he says: "The acquisition of the
country through which you are to pass
has inspired the country generally with
a great deal of interest in your enterprise." (a) Thus indicating that the
country which Lewis and Clark were
to explore had been acquired by the
United States.

The first sentence of the History of
Lewis and Clark's Expedition "on
the acquisition of Louisiana in the year
1803, April 30th, the attention of the
Government of the United States was
earnestly directed towards exploring
the entire territory" also clearly indi-
cates that the purpose was to explore
a territory supposed to have been acquired by the United States. (b)

(a) Lewis & Clark's Expedition, Vol. 1. p. XXIII.
(Coues' Edition.)

(b) Lewis & Clark's Expedition—Coues' Edition.
Vol. 1, p. 1.

In the "Preface by the Publisher" to the Journal of Patrick Gass, "one of the persons employed in the expedition" of Lewis and Clark, it is said, in speaking of the country explored, that "it will not be forgotten that an immense sum of treasure has been expended in the purchase of this country, and that it is now considered as belonging to the United States." (*a*)

Jefferson, in his message of January 18, 1803, before the purchase, and when France had acquired Louisiana from Spain, says: "The nation claiming the territory (Spain) regarding this as a literary pursuit which it is in the habit of permitting within its dominions, would not be disposed to view it with jealousy, even if the expiring state of its interests there did not render it a matter of indifference." And this also clearly shows that he then considered the country to be explored as a part of Louisiana. (*b*)

As stated, the boundary of the country acquired was uncertain and might

(*a*) Journal of Patrick Gass, p. VII–Pittsburg, 1807.
(*b*) Messages and Papers of the Presidents, Vol. 1, p. 354.

become a matter of dispute, but that Jefferson intended, by this exploration, to claim as a part of the Louisiana Purchase all that France ever claimed, cannot be denied. At the same time it is evident that our claim was carefully advanced, so as not needlessly to antagonize Spain, who was much dissatisfied with the treaty. In his message he cautiously says: "The appropriation of $2500 'for the purpose of extending the external commerce of the United States,' while understood and considered by the Executive as giving the Legislative sanction, would cover the undertaking from notice and prevent the obstructions which interested individuals might otherwise previously prepare in its way." (a)

In his message of December, 1805, Jefferson complains that Spain, west of the Mississippi River, claimed as a boundary "a line which would have left us but a string of land on that bank of the River Mississippi." (b)

(a) See Messages and Papers of the Presidents, Vol. 1, p. 354.

(b) See Messages and Papers of the Presidents, Vol. 1, p. 389.

His wisdom in at once causing our new acquisition to be explored and mapped in every direction was fully vindicated by subsequent events, and especially the expedition of Lewis and Clark across the Rocky Mountains to the Pacific Ocean. It is almost certain that if Jefferson had taken the narrow view as to the boundaries of Louisiana that are advanced by some now, with so much confidence, that the northwest coast would have fallen into the hands of England. A vast majority of the people of the United States then placed no value on the trans-montane country, and the broad claim made for the Pacific as a Louisiana boundary was ridiculed, by many, because the country was considered worthless and too remote.

In February, 1806, in a special message, Jefferson advised Congress of the success of the expedition of Lewis and Clark, and that the exploring party had passed the winter at the Mandans, about 1600 miles above the mouth of the Missouri, and to which point the Spanish Government caused the river to be mapped by Evans. Also that the country further west, between the Missouri and the Pacific, from the 34th to the 54th degree of latitude, had been crossed, and he transmitted a statistical view "of the Indian nations inhabiting the territory of Louisiana and the country adjacent to its northern and western borders, of their commerce, and other interesting circumstances respecting them." (a)

According to Martin, "Since the French enjoyed the undisputed possession of Louisiana, its extent in their opinion had scarcely any bounds to the northwest; and its limits were ill defined everywhere, except on the sea coast. As its sovereign claimed all the neighboring country, which was without inhabitants or occupied by savage enemies, the demarcation of its limits was impossible, even if it had been desirable." But he states erroneously, that by the Nootka Convention, Spain ceded to England the northwest coast as far south as the boundary of California and says, that

(a) Messages and Papers of the Presidents, Vol. 1, p. 398.

"where New Albion ended Louisiana was said to begin." (*a*) By the Nootka Convention no territorial rights were ceded to Great Britain, and consequently New Albion, by which name English geographers designated the whole northwest coast, was not extended south to the boundary of California, as Judge Martin supposed. All Spain ceded by the Nootka Convention was that the subjects of Great Britain should not be disturbed or molested in navigating or fishing on the Pacific or Southern Ocean, or in landing on the coasts of those seas in places not already occupied for the purpose of carrying on their commerce with the natives or making settlements. These rights up to 1790 Spain claimed exclusively in regard to the Pacific and Southern Oceans and by this convention ceded to Great Britain. The war however, of 1796 between Spain and Great Britain abrogated the convenvion. (*b*).

(*a*) Martin's History of Louisiana, Vol. 2, p. 201.

(*b*) See Greenhow's Oregon, p. 318, where the subject is fully and exhaustively discussed, and it is clearly shown that by the Nootka Convention Great Britain acquired no territorial rights.

Generally at the time of the acquisition the "colony and province" of Louisiana was considered to extend indefinitely west. Brackenridge says: "To the westward no limits were ever assigned by the French while they possessed Louisiana, but it was considered as including at least all the country whose streams either directly or indirectly discharged themselves into the Mississippi." (a) But when Brackenridge published his work in 1813 he admitted that then "our geographers had boldly claimed to the Pacific." Although he was not prepared to go so far, he says "that our right is much better supported than that of any other nation by reason of our exploring expedition and our establishments for trading with the Indians."

John Mason Peck, an able and distinguished writer on all subjects relating to the history of the west, also says, that by the aquisition of Louisiana the United States "extended her boundaries to the Pacific Ocean." (b)

(a) Brackenridge's Views of Louisiana, p. 61.
(b) See Annals of the West, page 534.

73

And again, that in Upper Louisiana was included "all the vast regions of the West, far as the Pacific Ocean, south of the 49th degree of north latitude unclaimed by Spain." (a)

In reply to the counter statement made by the British Minister, Packenham, in 1844, who in it quoted the letter of Jefferson to Breckenridge defining the boundaries of Louisiana on the west, Calhoun said: "It is manifest from the extract itself that the object of Mr. Jefferson was not to state the extent of the claim acquired with Louisiana, but simply to state how far its unquestioned boundaries extended; and those he limited westwardly by the Rocky Mountains. It is in like manner manifest from the document, as cited by the counterstatement, that his object was not to deny that our claims extend to the territory, but simply expressed his opinion of the impolicy of in the then state of our relations with Spain of bringing them forward. This so far from denying that we had claims admits them by

(a) Annals of the West, page 542.

the clearest implication. If indeed in either case his opinion had been equiv - ocally expressed, the prompt measure adopted by him to explore the territory after the treaty was negotiated, but before it was ratified, clearly shows that it was his opinion not only that we had acquired claims to it, but very important claims which deserved prompt attention." (a)

But it is said that the first descrip - tion of the western boundary of Louis - iana of any authority is the grant of September 17, 1712, made by Louis XIV to Crozat—and that the western limits fixed by this grant must control the territorial limits. The grant em - powered Crozat "to carry on the ex - clusive trade in all the territories by us possessed and bounded by New Mexico and those of the English in Carolina. All the establishments, posts, harbors, rivers, and especially the post and harbor of Dauphine Island, formerly called Massacre Island, the River St. Louis, formerly called the Mississippi, from the seashore to the Illinois, to-

(a) Calhoun's Works, Vol. 5, p. 454.

gether with the River St. Phillip, formerly called the Missouri River, and the St. Jerome, formerly called the Wabash (the Ohio), with all the countries, territories, lakes inland, and the rivers emptying directly or indirectly into that part of the River St. Louis. *** All the said territories, countries, streams and islands we will to be and remain comprised under the name of the 'Government of Louisiana,' which shall be dependent on the general government of New France and remain subordinate to it; and we will, moreover, that all the territories which we possess on this side of the Illinois be united as far as need to be to the general Government of New France and form a part thereof, reserving to ourselves to increase, if we think proper, the extent of the Government of Louisiana.'' (a) By the boundaries thus set forth the entire watershed of the Mississippi was included in the Territory of Louisiana. Unquestionably the territory and government thus created did not extend

(a) Wallace—Louisiana and Illinois under French Rule, p. 235.

beyond the Rocky Mountains, because that great range divides the waters flowing into the Pacific from those flowing into the Atlantic; but this ought not be construed to mean that France did not claim at a later date that Louisiana extended to the Pacific, or that the rights of France were limited and curtailed by the western mountains.

One salient fact already pointed out in support of the contention that Louisiana reached to the shores of the Pacific is unqualifiedly admitted by Marbois, namely, that the Bishopric of Louisiana was bounded by that ocean. (a)

It is also certain that the limits of Louisiana as originally defined in 1712 in the grant to Sieur Crozat, were not intended by the French king to be the final boundaries of the "colony or province," because in the first article defining the powers, duties and restrictions imposed on Crozat, it is expressly provided that the King reserves the liberty "of enlarging as we

(a) Ante page 56.

77

shall think fit, the extent of the government of the said country of Louisiana.'' Accordingly, as we have seen in 1717, the Illinois country was detached from Canada and added to Louisiana. The proces-verbal of LaSalle claiming the entire valley of the Mississippi, with all its affluents as well as all the country to the mouth of the Rio de Palmas (a river about 100 leagues from the River Panuco, Tampico, Mexico) no more defined the final limits of the boundaries of Louisiana, and such as those boundaries might finally become, than the grant to Sieur Crozat. The whole water-shed of the Mississippi was claimed both at the village of Kapaha, on the 14th of March, 1682, and at the mouth of the Mississippi on the 19th of April, 1682. But on the 14th of June, 1671, St. Lusson, at St. Marys of the Falls, as we have seen, took possession of all the ''countries, rivers, lakes and tribu-taries contiguous and adjacent thereun-to, as well discovered as to be discov-ered, which are bounded on the one side by the Northern and Western Seas and on the other side by the South Sea, including all its length and breadth," and accordingly as has been shown on several maps the limits of Louisiana were carried beyond the sources of the Mississippi to the basin of Lake Winnipeg, and even as far as the highlands encircling Hudson Bay. The claim of the territory thus added to the "colony or province of Louisiana" must be found not in the proces-verbal as promulgated by LaSalle, or the limits of Louisiana as defined by the grant to Crozat, but in the claim made by St. Lusson for France in 1671 as well. Also it should be remembered that the colonial ministers of the French king objected to the dots defining the limits of the "colony or province of Louisiana" on French maps, because boundaries thus indicated might furnish arguments to foreign powers inimical to French claims and pretensions. (a)

Again, when by treaty between Great Britain and France, Canada

(a) Ante, page 14.

with all its dependencies was ceded to Great Britain in 1763, the boundaries between the Hudson Bay territories ceded by treaty of Utrecht, 1713, and Louisiana remained undetermined. (*a*)

By the treaty of 1763 France ceded "in full right Canada with all its dependencies," and Great Britain "in order to establish peace on solid and durable foundations and to remove forever all subjects of dispute with regard to the limits of the British and French territories on the continent of America" agreed that in future "the boundaries between the dominions of his Britanic Majesty and those of his most Christain Majesty in that part of the world shall be fixed irrevocably by a line drawn along the middle of the River Mississippi from its source to the River Iberville, etc." Hence, it is claimed as we have seen by Falconer that Louisiana only extends as far north as the source of the Mississippi, 47 degrees, 30 minutes north, and then west to the mountains, (*b*) and not to the 49th parallel as universally understood and claimed.

(*a*) See Greenhow's Oregon, p. 140.
(*b*) On the Mississippi and Oregon, p. 61.

The theory, however, that the "colony and province of Louisiana" embraced the limits defined by the water-shed of the Mississippi and its tributaries was early denied by Great Britain, and in the interest of her settlements on the Atlantic coast. England claimed for its settlements specific limits along the coasts or bays on which English settlements were formed, and an extension across the the entire continent to the Pacific Ocean. A map published in Paris in 1757 clearly shows that the French fully understood the from sea-to-sea character of the English pretensions— heavy black lines running across the continent, showing the north and south limits of Virginia and other colonies, and that these pretensions conflicted with the French and Spanish claims to the "western sea" as the boundary of their possessions. This map is entitled "Carte des Pretentions des Anglois dans l'Amerique Septentrion-ale suivant leurs Chartres tant sur les possessions de la France que sur celles de l'Espagne." (a) These conflicting claims led to the struggle between France and England in America, and in that struggle the doctrine of England for an extension indefinitely west across the continent was victorious— the right of continuity prevailed over the theory of the water-shed.

By the treaty of 1763 the Mississippi, as we have seen, was made the permanent boundary between the possessions of Great Britian and France on this continent, and according to Calhoun this treaty "in effect extinguishes in favor of France whatever claim Great Britain may have had to the region west of the Mississippi."

In his reply to Packenham, Calhoun says that Great Britian by the treaty of 1763 fixing the Mississippi "as an irrevocable boundary between the territories of France and Great Britain," thereby surrendered to France all her claims on this continent west of the river, including, of course, those within the charter limits of her three colonies

(a)   See copy of map in Winsor's Mississippi Basin, p. 320.

which extend to the Pacific Ocean "on these united with those of France as the possessor of Louisiana we rest our claim of continuity as extending to that ocean without an opposing claim, except that of Spain, which we have since acquired and consequently removed by the treaty of Florida." (a)

The purchase of Louisiana restored and vested in the United States all claims acquired by France, and surrendered by Great Britain under the treaty of 1763, to the country west of the Mississippi. Certain it is that France had the same right of continuity in virtue of the possession of Louisiana, and the extinguishment of all rights of Great Britain by that treaty to the whole country west of the Rocky Mountains and lying west of Louisiana, if not embraced in the original limits of the "colony or province" as against Spain or England, which England had to the country west of the Allegheny Mountains as against France, with this difference,

(a) Calhoun's Works, Vol. 5, p. 453.

that Spain had nothing to oppose to the claim of France at the time, but the right of discovery. (*a*)

On the ground of contiguity principally Great Britain claimed the country west of the Alleghenies, enforced by other considerations. (*b*) And the strongest of these considerations was, that it could not consist with natural law, that the English colonies with a population of nearly two millions should be confined to a narrow belt of land between the Allegheny Mountains and the Atlantic, and that the right derived from the discovery of the main river should be carried to such an extent as to allow the French colonies with a population of only 50,000 to claim the whole valley of the Mississippi. (*c*)

So that the statement of Gallatin that the claims of the United States to the Northwest coast "dates at least from the time when they acquired Louisiana," cannot be denied.

(*a*)   Calhoun's Works, Vol. 5, p. 434.
(*b*)   Writings of Gallatin, 3rd Vol., p. 505.
(*c*)   Writings of Gallatin, 3rd Vol., p. 504.

"It is, therefore, not at all surprising that France should claim the country west of the Rocky Mountains (as may be inferred on her maps) on the same principle, that Great Britain had claimed and dispossessed her of the regions west of the Alleghenies, or that the United States as soon as they acquired the rights of France, should assert the same claim and take measures immediately after to explore it with a view to occupation and settlement." (a)

Great Britain for many years opposed our claim to the Northwest boundary in its entirety as far south as the mouth of the Columbia. It is supposed that Sir Alexander McKenzie, a man of great ability, great enterprise and wonderful energy inspired the English Government with the thought to claim the whole west coast of America as far south as the Columbia. (b) In 1793 McKenzie made his celebrated march of exploration across the Rocky Mountains, but missed the sources of the Columbia and fell upon the

(a) Calhoun's Works, Vol. 5, p. 435.
(b) Benton's Thirty Years, Vol. 1, p. 54.

Tacoutche Tesse, a north branch of the Frazier River, and following these waters in their course finally reached the Pacific Ocean five hundred miles north of the Columbia and also north of the 49th degree north latitude. It was not, however, until 1818 that the British Government for the first time made known the grounds upon which its pretensions to the northwest coast rested, namely, the voyage of Capt. Cook, who in 1776 was directed to explore the coast of New Albion, a name which had been bestowed by Drake upon this coast when he sailed along it with one of his flying piratical squadrons. It was claimed that Cook's voyage gave Great Britain a right from discovery, as also purchases of land made by the English from the natives prior to the American Revolution. No formal proposition was made as to boundary, but it was intimated that the Columbia River was the most convenient boundary. (*a*)   To this proposition

(*a*)   Letters from Messrs. Gallatin and Rush, Oct. 28, 1320; Benton's Thirty Years, Vol. 1, p. 51.

our representatives would not assent, but it was agreed that the country on the northwest coast claimed by either party should without prejudice to the claims of either party for a limited time be left open for the purpose of trade to the inhabitants of both countries, and this agreement was embodied in the convention of 1818. Afterwards in 1827 this agreement was extended indefinitely, but to be cancelled upon twelve months' notice by either party.

In subsequent negotiations British agents further rested their claim upon the discovery of McKenzie, the seizure of Astoria during the war of 1812, the Nootka Sound treaty of 1790. Of the grounds thus advanced not one could be considered tenable. Cook never saw, much less took possession of the northwest coast. The Indians from whom British subjects were said to have purchased prior to the Revolution were not even named and the transaction was in no wise identified, only that it took place at the mouth of the Columbia. McKenzie did not discover the Columbia, but the Frazier River five hundred miles north. The seizure of Astoria gave no title by conquest. In addition, Astoria was at the close of the war restored, and the treaty of Nootka of 1790 was in no wise a treaty of acquisition. (a)

After great agitation for many years, notice was finally given by the United States to abrogate the convention of 1827, and in 1846 a treaty was made and ratified fixing the 49th degree parallel north latitude as the boundary line between the United States and England, deflecting, however, through the Straits of Fuca instead of dividing Vancouver Island, this being the boundary which for a period of forty years had been tendered to the Government of Great Britain, in 1807 by Jefferson; in 1824 by Monroe; in 1826 by Adams; in 1842 by Tyler and which in 1845 finally was accepted when presented by Polk. "Thus the ancient boundary fixed by the treaty of Utrecht between England and France was finally adopted," a boundary charac-

(a) Benton's Thirty Years, Vol. 1, p. 51.

terized by Benton as "wonderfully adapted to the natural divisions of the country, separating the two systems of water, those of the Columbia and Frazier Rivers as natural and commodiously on the west of the mountains as it parted on the east side of the same mountains the two systems of water which belonged on the one hand to the Gulf of Mexico, and on the other to the Hudson Bay or Arctic Ocean. That at the treaty of Utrecht with but imperfect geographical knowledge, such a line so long and so straight and so adapted to the rights of all parties should have been selected as the boundary line of Louisiana on the north is one of the marvels of history."

Although manifest that the Louisiana Purchase secured us the coast, we find that some would rest the title of the United States on the so-called discovery of the Columbia by Capt. Gray. No doubt Gray's discovery, or re-discovery, of the Columbia was an incident in the Oregon controversy, but the mouth of the Columbia was discovered by Heceta prior to Gray, and the coast taken possession of in the name of Spain. Before Gray entered the river the entire coast had been traced, and Gray neither discovered it for the first time nor had authority to take possession of it. In the discovery he had been anticipated by Heceta. The re-discovery by Capt. Gray undoubtedly added strength to the claim of the United States, but it was the Louisiana Purchase that gave us title to the territory and made Gray's entrance and voyage up the Columbia important as well as the fact that he gave the river the name of his ship "Columbia."

The expedition of Lewis and Clark, without the possession of the Louisiana hinterland, would have given the world some valuable geographical and topographical information, but in no wise would have given title to the territory to the United States. The expedition was sent out to secure trade and commerce, and it is manifest that the territory as far as the Pacific was considered by Jefferson and his contemporaries as an unexplored portion of Louisiana. The expedition of Lewis and Clark "brought to the knowledge of the world this great river, the greatest by far on the western side of the continent. * * * It clearly entitled us to the claim of priority of discovery as to its head branches and the exploration of the river and the region through which it passes, as the voyage of Capt. Gray and the Spanish navigator Heceta, entitled us to priority in reference to its mouth and the entrance into its channel." (a)

The claim of the United States to the possession of the territory west of the Rocky Mountains between the 42nd and 49th parallels of latitude was by Gallatin well and ably placed on the ground:

First—Of the acquisition by the United States of the titles of France through the Louisiana treaty, and the titles of Spain through the Florida treaty.

Second—The discovery of the mouth of the Columbia. The first

(a) Calhoun's Works, Vol. 5, p. 430.

exploration of the country through which that river flows, and the establishments of the first settlements in those countries by American citizens. The virtual recognition of the titles of the United States by the British government in the restitution agreeable to the first article of the treaty of Ghent, of the post near the mouth of the Columbia which had been taken during the war; and

Lastly—Upon the ground of contiguity, which would give the United States a stronger right to those territories than could be advanced by any other power, a doctrine always maintained by Great Britain from the period of her earliest attempts at colonization in America, as clearly proved by her charters in which the whole breadth of the continent between certain parallels of latitude established at points on the borders of the Atlantic. "If," says Mr. Gallatin, "some trading factories on the shores of Hudson Bay have been considered by Great Britain as giving an exclusive right of occupancy as far as the Rocky Mountains, if the infant settlement on the more southern Atlantic justified a claim thence to the South Seas, and which was actually enforced to the Mississippi, that of the millions already within reach of those seas cannot consistently be rejected." (a)

General Walker, director of the 10th census, says: "The discovery and exploration of the Columbia River by Capt. Gray, an American, the purchase of Louisiana and all that belonged to it as far as the Pacific, from the French in 1803, their claim being the next best to that of Spain, the exploration of the Columbia by Lewis and Clark, and the treaty of limits concluded between Spain and the United States in 1819, by which the territory north of the 42nd degree north latitude was expressly declared to belong to us, constitute our title to these regions." (b)

(a) Greenhow's Oregon, p. 348. Our well founded claim grounded on continuity has greatly been strengthened by the rapid increase of population in the Mississippi Valley. Calhoun's Works, Vol. 5, page 439.

(b) Vol. 9, 10th Census, p. 23.

In this paragraph our title to the northwest coast is correctly but confusedly stated. Our title primarily rested on the Louisiana Purchase. The United States "acquired from France by treaty of Louisiana important and substantial claims to the territory" on the northwest coast west of the Rocky Mountains. (*a*)

It is certain that by the purchase of Louisiana the United States first became a power on the Pacific Ocean. Gray's re-discovery of the Columbia was made valuable by the Louisiana Purchase. Without that purchase his entrance into the Columbia and navigation of that river would have given us no rights.

The discoveries of Spain while in possession of Louisiana clearly inured to the benefit of France, wherever such explorations enlarged the limits of the "province or colony of Louisiana," or made the limits and boundaries of that colony more certain and definite. And the voyages and discoveries of Perez and of Heceta en-

(*a*) Calhoun's Works, Vol. 5, p. 554.

larged and made more certain those
limits and must be considered as en-
uring to the benefit of the "colony or
province."

But by the treaty of 1818 all the
rights of Spain north of the 42nd parallel were granted to us, thus making
absolutely certain the boundaries of
the Louisiana Purchase on the south
to the Pacific Ocean.

The exedition of Lewis and Clark
was sent out to explore the unexplored regions of the Louisiana Purchase, and when the exploring party
reached the western ocean, erected
the rude Fort Clatsop at the mouth of
the Columbia and raised the flag of the
United States, it was notice to all the
world that we had taken possession
of the farthest limits of the Louisiana
Purchase, and that a new power was
established on the shores of the Pacific,
for no one can contend that this expedition without the purchase of the
"colony or province of Loulsiana"
could or would have resulted in the
acquisition of territorial rights.

"When this expedition started out

on its celebrated march," says the late Dr. Elliott Coues, who has so well edited and annotated the narrative of this great expedition, "Louisiana was all that country which was ceded by Spain to France and by the latter to the United States. It was practically the United States west of the Mississippi. A map of the period just before the cession would show: United States east of the Mississippi; British possessions north of the 49th degree and along the Great Lakes, etc.; Spanish possessions on the southwest up to about the 38th degree at the point of the farthest northward extension, the rest being Louisiana. A straight line from the Straits of Fuca on the Pacific coast to the mouth of the Mississippi River would run through 'Louisiana' from the northwest to the southeast. Such was the vast area acquired by the United States through Jefferson's magnificent stroke." (a)

So whatever the different arguments that may at this late day be

(a) Coues' Edition Lewis and Clark's Expedition, Vol. 1, p. XXXIII.

brought forward, principally borrowed from British sources, it is clear that all of Montana and the states of Idaho, Oregon and Washington should be placed in the galaxy of the Louisiana Purchase states.

The First American Frontier

AN ARNO PRESS/NEW YORK TIMES COLLECTION

Agnew, Daniel.
A History of the Region of Pennsylvania North of the Allegheny River. 1887.

Alden, George H.
New Government West of the Alleghenies Before 1780. 1897.

Barrett, Jay Amos.
Evolution of the Ordinance of 1787. 1891.

Billon, Frederick.
Annals of St. Louis in its Early Days Under the French and Spanish Dominations. 1886.

Billon, Frederick.
Annals of St. Louis in its Territorial Days, 1804-1821. 1888.

Littel, William.
Political Transactions in and Concerning Kentucky. 1926.

Bowles, William Augustus.
Authentic Memoirs of William Augustus Bowles. 1916.

Bradley, A. G.
The Fight with France for North America. 1900.

Brannan, John, ed.
Official Letters of the Military and Naval Officers of the War, 1812-1815. 1823.

Brown, John P.
Old Frontiers. 1938.

Brown, Samuel R.
The Western Gazetteer. 1817.

Cist, Charles.
**Cincinnati Miscellany of Antiquities of the West and Pioneer
History.** (2 volumes in one). 1845-6.

Claiborne, Nathaniel Herbert.
**Notes on the War in the South with Biographical Sketches
of the Lives of Montgomery, Jackson, Sevier, and Others.**
1819.

Clark, Daniel.
Proofs of the Corruption of Gen. James Wilkinson. 1809.

Clark, George Rogers.
**Colonel George Rogers Clark's Sketch of His Campaign in
the Illinois in 1778-9.** 1869.

Collins, Lewis.
Historical Sketches of Kentucky. 1847.

Cruikshank, Ernest, ed,
**Documents Relating to Invasion of Canada and the
Surrender of Detroit.** 1912.

Cruikshank, Ernest, ed,
**The Documentary History of the Campaign on the Niagara
Frontier, 1812-1814.** (4 volumes). 1896-1909.

Cutler, Jervis.
**A Topographical Description of the State of Ohio, Indian
Territory, and Louisiana.** 1812.

Cutler, Julia P.
The Life and Times of Ephraim Cutler. 1890.

Darlington, Mary C.
**History of Col. Henry Bouquet and the Western Frontiers
of Pennsylvania.** 1920.

Darlington, Mary C.
Fort Pitt and Letters From the Frontier. 1892.

De Schweinitz, Edmund.
The Life and Times of David Zeisberger. 1870.

Dillon, John B.
History of Indiana. 1859.

Eaton, John Henry.
Life of Andrew Jackson. 1824.

English, William Hayden.
Conquest of the Country Northwest of the Ohio. (2 volumes in one). 1896.

Flint, Timothy.
Indian Wars of the West. 1833.

Forbes, John.
Writings of General John Forbes Relating to His Service in North America. 1938.

Forman, Samuel S.
Narrative of a Journey Down the Ohio and Mississippi in 1789-90. 1888.

Haywood, John.
Civil and Political History of the State of Tennessee to 1796. 1823.

Heckewelder, John.
History, Manners and Customs of the Indian Nations. 1876.

Heckewelder, John.
Narrative of the Mission of the United Brethren. 1820.

Hildreth, Samuel P.
Pioneer History. 1848.

Houck, Louis.
The Boundaries of the Louisiana Purchase: A Historical Study. 1901.

Houck, Louis.
History of Missouri. (3 volumes in one). 1908.

Houck, Louis.
The Spanish Regime in Missouri. (2 volumes in one). 1909.

Jacob, John J.
A Biographical Sketch of the Life of the Late Capt. Michael Cresap. 1826.

Jones, David.
A Journal of Two Visits Made to Some Nations of Indians
on the West Side of the River Ohio, in the Years 1772 and
1773. 1774.

Kenton, Edna.
Simon Kenton. 1930.

Loudon, Archibald.
Selection of Some of the Most Interesting Narratives of
Outrages. (2 volumes in one). 1808-1811.

Monette, J. W.
History, Discovery and Settlement of the Mississippi Valley.
(2 volumes in one). 1846.

Morse, Jedediah.
American Gazetteer. 1797.

Pickett, Albert James.
History of Alabama. (2 volumes in one). 1851.

Pope, John.
A Tour Through the Southern and Western Territories. 1792.

Putnam, Albigence Waldo.
History of Middle Tennessee. 1859.

Ramsey, James G. M.
Annals of Tennessee. 1853.

Ranck, George W.
Boonesborough. 1901.

Robertson, James Rood, ed.
Petitions of the Early Inhabitants of Kentucky to the Gen.
Assembly of Virginia. 1914.

Royce, Charles.
Indian Land Cessions. 1899.

Rupp, I. Daniel.
History of Northampton, Lehigh, Monroe, Carbon and
Schuykill Counties. 1845.

Safford, William H.
The Blennerhasset Papers. 1864.

St. Clair, Arthur.
A Narrative of the Manner in which the Campaign Against the Indians, in the Year 1791 was Conducted. 1812.

Sargent, Winthrop, ed.
A History of an Expedition Against Fort DuQuesne in 1755. 1855.

Severance, Frank H.
An Old Frontier of France. (2 volumes in one). 1917.

Sipe, C. Hale.
Fort Ligonier and Its Times. 1932.

Stevens, Henry N.
Lewis Evans: His Map of the Middle British Colonies in America. 1920.

Timberlake, Henry.
The Memoirs of Lieut. Henry Timberlake. 1927.

Tome, Philip.
Pioneer Life: Or Thirty Years a Hunter. 1854.

Trent, William.
Journal of Captain William Trent From Logstown to Pickawillany. 1871.

Walton, Joseph S.
Conrad Weiser and the Indian Policy of Colonial Pennsylvania. 1900.

Withers, Alexander Scott.
Chronicles of Border Warfare. 1895.